William Channing Gannett, Frederick Lucian Hosmer

The Thought of God in Hymns and Poems

Second Series

William Channing Gannett, Frederick Lucian Hosmer

The Thought of God in Hymns and Poems
Second Series

ISBN/EAN: 9783744704922

Printed in Europe, USA, Canada, Australia, Japan

Cover: Foto ©Lupo / pixelio.de

More available books at **www.hansebooks.com**

THE THOUGHT OF GOD

IN

HYMNS AND POEMS

Second Series

By the Same Authors.

THE THOUGHT OF GOD IN HYMNS AND POEMS. *First Series.* 16mo. Cloth, $1.00; paper, 50 cents.

THE
THOUGHT OF GOD
IN
HYMNS AND POEMS

Second Series

BY

FREDERICK L. HOSMER
AND
WILLIAM C. GANNETT

BOSTON
ROBERTS BROTHERS
1894

Copyright, 1894

BY FREDERICK L. HOSMER AND
WILLIAM C. GANNETT

University Press
JOHN WILSON AND SON, CAMBRIDGE

CONTENTS

		PAGE
One Law, One Life, One Love	F. L. H.	9
'Who Wert and Art and Evermore Shalt Be'	W. C. G.	11
In Lonely Vigil	F. L. H.	13
Edelweiss: *Translation*	"	14
Edelweiss	"	15
The Crowning Day	W. C. G.	16
The Day of God	F. L. H.	18
The Inward Witness	"	20
Thou who art Strong to Heal	"	22
The Heavenly Helper	"	24
Church-Bells	W. C. G.	26
Sun-Gleams	"	29
The Grace of God	F. L. H.	30
In Littles	W. C. G.	31
With Self Dissatisfied	F L. H.	33
Behind and Before	"	35
'Think on These Things'	"	38
The Cross on the Flag	"	40

CONTENTS

		PAGE
From Generation to Generation	F. L. H.	42
Holy Places	"	44
The Building of the Temple	W. C. G.	46
The Word of God	"	48
Unto Him All Live	F. L. H.	50
Easter Morn	"	51
Risen	"	52
What will the Violets be	W. C. G.	54
Over the Land in Glory	F. L. H.	55
Easter Festival	"	57
Discipleship	"	59
The Man of Nazareth	"	62
Mary's Manger-Song	W. C. G.	64
Whittier	F. L. H.	66
Whittier	W. C. G.	67
'Nothing but a Poet'	"	68
Rembrandt	F. L. H.	70
The Sower	"	72
John C. Learned	"	75
'Incarnate Cheer'	W. C. G.	76
Thirty Thousand	"	77
Golden Wedding	"	79
Twilight	"	82
'Death as Friend'	"	84
A. L. G.	"	87
Alma Mater	F. L. H.	89
The Village Meeting-House	"	91

CONTENTS

		PAGE
The Days	W. C. G.	95
The Old Love-Song	"	97
The Dear Togetherness	"	99
Hero by Brevet	"	101
Nursery Logic	"	103
How Little Jo Named the Baby	F. L. H.	106
In the Albula Pass	"	109
Coronado Beach	"	111
Dover	W. C. G.	112
We See as we Are	"	114
Tree-Surprise	"	115
A Day in October	F. L. H.	117

ONE LAW, ONE LIFE, ONE LOVE

O Prophet souls of all the years,
   Bend o'er us from above;
Your far-off vision, toils and tears
   Now to fulfilment move!

From tropic clime and zones of frost
   They come, of every name,—
This, this our day of Pentecost,
   The Spirit's tongue of flame!

The ancient barriers disappear:
   Down bow the mountains high;
The sea-divided shores draw near
   In a world's unity.

One Life together we confess,
   One all-indwelling Word,
One holy Call to righteousness
   Within the silence heard:

10 ONE LAW, ONE LIFE, ONE LOVE

One Law that guides the shining spheres
   As on through space they roll,
And speaks in flaming characters
   On Sinais of the soul:

One Love, unfathomed, measureless,
   An ever-flowing sea,
That holds within its vast embrace
   Time and eternity.

World's Parliament of Religions
   CHICAGO, 1893

'WHO WERT AND ART AND EVERMORE SHALT BE'

BRING, O Morn, thy music! Bring, O
　　Night, thy hushes!
Oceans, laugh the rapture to the storm-winds
　　coursing free!
Suns and stars are singing, Thou art our
　　Creator,
　　Who wert and art and evermore shalt
　　　be!

Life and Death, thy creatures, praise thee,
　　Mighty Giver!
Praise and prayer are rising in thy beast
　　and bird and tree:
Lo! they praise and vanish, vanish at thy
　　bidding,—
　　Who wert and art and evermore shalt
　　　be!

Light us! lead us! love us! cry thy grop-
    ing nations,
Pleading in the thousand tongues but nam-
    ing only thee,
Weaving blindly out thy holy, happy pur-
    pose, —
    Who wert and art and evermore shalt
        be!

Life nor Death can part us, O thou Love
    Eternal,
Shepherd of the wandering star and souls
    that wayward flee!
Homeward draws the spirit to thy Spirit
    yearning, —
    Who wert and art and evermore shalt
        be!

1893

IN LONELY VIGIL

O THOU in lonely vigil led
To follow Truth's new-risen star
Ere yet her morning skies are red,
And vale and upland shadowed are, —

Gird up thy loins and take thy road,
Obedient to the vision be :
Trust not in numbers ; God is God,
And one with Him majority !

Soon pass the judgments of the hour,
Forgotten are the scorn and blame ;
The Word moves on, a gladdening power,
And safe enshrines the prophet's fame,

Now, as of old, in lowly plight
The Christ of larger faith is born :
The watching shepherds come by night,
And then — the kings of earth at morn !

Emerson Commemoration, W. U. C., 1888

EDELWEISS

From the German of Hermann Lingg

On the rock and girt with ice,
    Neighbor to the circling star,
Bloomest thou, dear edelweiss,
    From all other flowers afar;
By their joyous spring unblest,
Lonely on the rock's cold breast.

Where the lightnings have their home,
    And the startled chamois listen,
Where the plunging waters foam,
    Eagles reign, and glaciers glisten, —
Death and terror everywhere, —
Pure and glad thou bloomest there.

So stands he in noble pain,
    Lone anear the arching heaven,
Lonely proud, who worldly gain,
    Smiles and honors, all has given
Freely as his freedom's price, —
As thou bloomest, edelweiss!

1891

EDELWEISS

This edelweiss I wear was not first mine;
I had it cheaply in the little town
Of one who from the mountains had come
    down;
A meek-eyed man, rough-clad, with many a
    sign
Of burning sun and of the tempest's frown.
Now through the valley, with its corn and
    wine,
His star-blooms badge the thronging tourists
    fine
Whose feet his toilsome path have never
    known.

O prophet souls, who with bruised feet have
    trod
The heaven-lit heights and thence to us have
    brought
Your wider vision, your high-hearted faith,
Your hope for Man, your larger thought of
    God, —
We wear your edelweiss; Life's common lot
Ever to your high service witnesseth!

SWITZERLAND, 1888

THE CROWNING DAY

THE morning hangs its signal
   Upon the mountain's crest,
While all the sleeping valleys
   In silent darkness rest;
From peak to peak it flashes,
   It laughs along the sky
That the crowning day is coming by and by!
Chorus: O, the crowning day is coming,
      Is coming by and by!
   We can see the rose of morning,
      A glory in the sky.
   And that splendor on the hill-tops
      O'er all the land shall lie
   In the crowning day that's coming
      by and by!

Above the generations
   The lonely prophets rise, —
The Truth flings dawn and day-star
   Within their glowing eyes;

From heart to heart it brightens,
  It draweth ever nigh,
Till it crowneth all men thinking, by and by!
Chorus: O, the crowning day is coming!

The soul hath lifted moments
  Above the drift of days,
When life's great meaning breaketh
  In sunrise on our ways;
From hour to hour it haunts us,
  The vision draweth nigh,
Till it crowneth living, *dying*, by and by!
Chorus: O, the crowning day is coming!

And in the sunrise standing,
  Our kindling hearts confess
That 'no good thing is failure,
  No evil thing success!'
From age to age it groweth,
  That radiant faith so high,
And its crowning day is coming by and by!
Chorus: O, the crowning day is coming!

Music: 'Gospel Hymns,' No. 416. 1886

THE DAY OF GOD

Thy kingdom come, — on bended knee
   The passing ages pray;
And faithful souls have yearned to see
   On earth that kingdom's day.

But the slow watches of the night
   Not less to God belong,
And for the everlasting Right
   The silent stars are strong.

And lo! already on the hills
   The flags of dawn appear;
Gird up your loins, ye prophet souls,
   Proclaim the day is near!

The day in whose clear-shining light
   All wrong shall stand revealed;
When justice shall be throned in might,
   And every hurt be healed:

When knowledge hand in hand with peace
  Shall walk the earth abroad, —
The day of perfect righteousness,
  The promised day of God!

M. T. S., June 12, 1891

THE INWARD WITNESS

O Thou whose Spirit witness bears
　　Within our spirits free
That we thy children are and heirs
　　Of thine eternity, —

Here may this simple faith sublime
　　O'er-arch us like the sky;
Secure below the drift of time
　　Its firm foundations lie.

Our thought o'erflows each written scroll,
　　Our creeds, they rise and fall;
The life of God within the soul
　　Lives and outlasts them all.

Here may that witness clearer grow
　　Each waiting heart within,
The way of filial duty show
　　And glad obedience win.

Here be life's sorrows sanctified,
  Here truth her radiance pour ;
While hope and faith and love abide,
  Forever more and more !

For T. K., OMAHA, 1891

THOU WHO ART STRONG TO HEAL

O Fount of Being's sea,
Forever flowing free,
   The One in all, —
Thou whom no eye e'er saw,
Indwelling Love and Law,
To thee we suppliant draw,
   On thee we call.

Be consecrate to truth,
In manhood as in youth,
   Our growing powers;
That we may read thy thought
Nature and Life inwrought,
Thy perfect will be taught,
   And make it ours!

Thine image may we own
In Man, creation's crown,
   These temples thine:

Holy our calling be,
From bonds of pain to free,
And bring the liberty
    Of life divine!

Thy presence still abide
Within these walls to guide,
    Inspire and bless;
Thou who art strong to heal,
The Christ-like touch reveal,
And in each spirit seal
    Thy tenderness!

Rush Medical College, CHICAGO, 1891

THE HEAVENLY HELPER

Unto thee, abiding ever,
    Look I in my need,
Strength of every good endeavor,
    Holy thought and deed!

Thou dost guide the stars of heaven,
    Heal the broken heart,
Bring in turn the morn and even, —
    Law and Love thou art.

Clouds and darkness are about thee,
    Just and sure thy throne, —
Not a sparrow falls without thee,
    All to thee is known.

Origin and end of being,
    All things in and through, —
Light thou art of all my seeing,
    Power to will and do.

Through my life, whate'er betide me,
  Thou my trust shalt be;
Whom have I on earth beside thee,
  Whom in heaven but thee?

1886

CHURCH-BELLS

Over hills and valleys,
   Over prairies wide,
Quiet call the church-bells
   To the altar-side.
High in old cathedrals
   Chant the brazen lips,
Down the leafy by-ways
   Airy pleading slips.

In his toil the worker
   Pauses at the sound, —
Heaven a little nearer,
   Earth a holier ground.
At the sound the Sundays
   With low music fill, —
Hark! the lands are singing,
   Then with prayers are still.

Softer than the church-bells
   With their mellow peal,
Softer, sweeter calling,
   Mystic voices steal;

All the shadowy valleys
  Memory calls her own,
All the spirit's hill-tops
  Listen for the tone.

Every soul that listens
  Hears the secret chime, —
Bells from quiet inlands
  Out of space or time;
Mother-tones will stir them,
  Child-appeals will start,
Hero-deeds will set them
  Ringing in the heart.

Matin calls of duty
  Wake us every day;
'Mid each happy labor
  Angelus says 'Pray!'
Every hour that passes
  Hath a vesper end,
Breathing, 'One who sleeps not
  Is thy constant Friend.'

Every hope that wings us,
    Making eagle-free,
Every shame that bows us,
    Every loyalty,
Each new joy and laughter,
    Sorrows old that bide, —
Are God's church-bells calling
    To an altar-side.

1891

SUN-GLEAMS

As silent as the sun-gleam in the forest,
    As quiet as the shadow on the hill,
Is the shining of the Spirit in our dimness,
    Is the falling of its calm upon our will.

But subtler than the sun-lift in the leaf-bud,
    That thrills through all the forests, making May,
And stronger than the strength that plants the mountains,
    Is that shining in the heart-lands, bringing day.

AUSABLE PONDS, 1889

THE GRACE OF GOD

'My grace is sufficient for thee'

'Mid my life's vicissitude,
Seeming evil mixed with good;
'Mid its pleasure and its pain,
Alternating loss and gain, —
Be thou still my staff and rod,
All-sustaining grace of God!

Like a pilgrim here I pass,
Darkly see as through a glass;
Little know I of the way,
What shall be I cannot say, —
Let thy light upon me shine,
All-sufficient grace divine!

'Mid my ever-changing mood
God who changeth not is good;
And his word within I have,
He will guard the life he gave, —
Sing, my soul, along thy road,
Happy in the grace of God.

1877

IN LITTLES

A LITTLE House of Life,
With many noises rife,
   Noises of joy and crime;
A little gate of birth
Through which I slipped to Earth
   And found myself in Time.

And there, not far before,
Another little door,
   One day to swing so free!
None pauses there to knock,
No other hand tries lock, —
   It knows, and waits for me.

From out what Silent Land
I came, on Earth to stand
   And learn life's little art,
Is not in me to say:
I know I did not stray, —
   Was *sent;* to come, my part.

And down what Silent Shore
Beyond yon little door
  I pass, I cannot tell;
I know I shall not stray,
Nor ever lose the way, —
  Am *sent;* and all is well.

1891

WITH SELF DISSATISFIED

Not when, with self dissatisfied,
   O Lord, I lowly lie,
So much I need thy grace to guide,
   And thy reproving eye, —

As when the sound of human praise
   Grows pleasant to my ear,
And in its light my broken ways
   Fair and complete appear.

By failure and defeat made wise,
   We come to know at length
What strength within our weakness lies,
   What weakness in our strength:

What inward peace is born of strife,
   What power, of being spent;
What wings unto our upward life
   Is noble discontent.

O Lord, we need thy shaming look
That burns all low desire;
The discipline of thy rebuke
Shall be refining fire!

1893

BEHIND AND BEFORE

'One thing I do; the things behind forgetting
    And reaching forward to the things before,
Unto the goal, the prize of God's high calling,
    Onward I press,' — said that great soul of yore.

And in the heart, like strains of martial music,
    Echo the words of courage, trust, and cheer,
The while we stand, half hoping, half regretting,
    Between the coming and the parting year.

Behind are joys, fond hopes that found fulfilment,
    Sweet fellowships, glad toil of hand and brain.

Unanswered prayers, burdens of loss and
    sorrow,
    Faces that look no more in ours again.

Before us lie the hills, sunlit with promise,
    Fairer fulfilments than the past could
    know,
New growths of soul, new leadings of the
    Spirit,
    And all the glad surprises God will show.

All we have done, or nobly failed in doing,
    All we have been, or bravely striven to be,
Makes for our gain, within us still surviving
    As power and larger possibility.

All, all shall count; the mingled joy and
    sorrow
    To force of finer being rise at last:
From the crude ores in trial's furnace smelted
    The image of the perfect life is cast.

'Onward I press, the things behind forget-
    ting
    And reaching forward to the things be-
    fore:'

Ring the brave words like strains of martial
    music
  As we pass through the New Year's
    opened door.

1890

'THINK ON THESE THINGS'

'Whatsoever things are true, whatsoever things are honorable, whatsoever things are just, whatsoever things are pure, whatsoever things are lovely, whatsoever things are of good report, if there be any virtue, and if there be any praise, think on these things.'

WHATSOEVER is just and pure,
    Think on these things, my soul!
Earth shall vanish, but these endure,
    Think on these things, my soul!
        When all else shall fail thee,
        These shall still avail thee;
Think on these things, strive for these things,
    Cherish these things, my soul!

Truth and honor, they call to thee,
    Think on these things, my soul!
What of virtue and praise there be,
    Think on these things, my soul!

  These have been the glory
   Of all human story;
Think on these things, strive for these things,
  Cherish these things, my soul!

Faithful spirits before have gone,
  Think on these things, my soul!
Grand thy heritage, hero-won,
  Think on these things, my soul!
   From all brave endeavor
   Springeth good forever;
Think on these things, strive for these things,
  Cherish these things, my soul!

 Music: 'Gospel Hymns,' No. 282

THE CROSS ON THE FLAG

From age to age they gather, all the brave of heart and strong,
In the strife of truth with error, of the right against the wrong;
I can see their gleaming banner, I can hear their triumph-song:
      The Truth is marching on!

' In this sign we conquer;' 't is the symbol of our faith,
Made holy by the might of love triumphant over death;
He finds his life who loseth it, forevermore it saith:
      The Right is marching on!

The earth is circling onward out of shadow into light;
The stars keep watch above our way, however dark the night;

For every martyr's stripe there glows a bar
    of morning bright :
        And Love is marching on !

Lead on, O cross of martyr-faith, with thee
    is victory !
Shine forth, O stars and reddening dawn,
    the full day yet shall be !
On earth his kingdom cometh, and with joy
    our eyes shall see :
        Our God is marching on !

For S. S. H., Decorah, Ia., 1891

FROM GENERATION TO GENERATION

O Light, from age to age the same,
    Forever living Word, —
Here have we felt thy kindling flame,
    Thy voice within have heard.

Here holy thought and hymn and prayer
    Have winged the spirit's powers,
And made these walls divinely fair, —
    Thy temple, Lord, and ours.

What visions rise above the years,
    What tender memories throng,
Till the eye fills with happy tears,
    The heart with grateful song!

Vanish the mists of time and sense;
    They come, the loved of yore,
And one encircling Providence
    Holds all for evermore.

O, not in vain their toil who wrought
  To build faith's freer shrine, —
Nor theirs whose steadfast love and thought
  Have watched the fire divine.

Burn, holy fire, and shine more wide!
  While systems rise and fall,
Faith, hope, and charity abide,
  The heart and soul of all.

<small>QUINCY, ILL.</small> : Fiftieth Anniversary, 1890

HOLY PLACES

Where men on mounts of vision
    Have passed the veil within,
Where hearts bowed in contrition
    Have risen from their sin,
Where light on upturned faces
    Earth's Calvaries has crowned, —
Here are her holy places,
    This, consecrated ground.

Where life is nobly given
    And man for man has died,
Where bonds of wrong are riven
    And right is glorified, —
One faith the spirit traces,
    Brightening from age to age;
These are earth's holy places
    And shrines of pilgrimage.

HOLY PLACES

Here, Lord, may thy revealing
   In waiting hearts be known,
Here holier thought and feeling
   The secret Presence own:
May prayer and aspiration,
   In-shinings of thy grace,
And sorrow's consolation
   Make this our holy place!

Still from the spirit's essence
   All things new meaning win;
The temple of thy presence
   Is ever, Lord, within.
May outward dedication
   Have inward seal and sign,
The spirit's consecration
   Make beautiful the shrine!

For C. W. W., OAKLAND, CAL., 1891

THE BUILDING OF THE TEMPLE

THE CORNER-STONE

He laid his rocks in courses,
   His forest crowned the hill,
He yoked the ancient forces
   And lent them to our will;
The heart he woke to duty,
   He graced the builder's thought,—
He gave Creation beauty,
   And he the Temple wrought!

Now, Father, build within us
   The Temple's counterpart,
Deep laid in holy purpose,
   Fair colored of the heart;
Its windows heaven-lighted,
   Peace and Good-will its plan,
Its towers our Faith and Worship,
   Its doors the Love of Man!

1888

THE DEDICATION

To cloisters of the spirit
    These aisles of quiet lead:
Here may the vision gladden,
    The voice within us plead!
And may the dear All-Father,
    Who maketh trouble cease,
Here send his two, the blessed,
    His angels Shame and Peace!

Here be no man a stranger;
    No holy cause be banned;
No good for one be counted
    Not good for all the land!
And here for prophet voices
    The message never fail, —
'God reigns! His Truth shall conquer,
    And Right and Love prevail!'

1894

THE WORD OF GOD

It sounds along the ages,
   Soul answering to soul;
It kindles on the pages
   Of every Bible scroll;
The psalmists heard and sang it,
   From martyr-lips it broke,
And prophet-tongues outrang it
   Till sleeping nations woke.

From Sinai's cliffs it echoed,
   It breathed from Buddha's tree,
It charmed in Athens' market,
   It gladdened Galilee;
The hammer-stroke of Luther,
   The Pilgrims' sea-side prayer,
The oracles of Concord,
   One holy Word declare.

It dates each new ideal, —
    Itself it knows not time;
Man's laws but catch the music
    Of its eternal chime.
It calls — and lo, new Justice!
    It speaks — and lo, new Truth!
In ever nobler stature
    And unexhausted youth.

It everywhere arriveth;
    Recks not of small and great;
It shapes the unborn atom,
    It tells the sun its fate.
The wing-beat of archangel
    Its boundary never nears:
Forever on it soundeth
    The music of the spheres!

1894

UNTO HIM ALL LIVE

O Lord of Life, where'er they be,
Safe in thine own eternity,
Our dead are living unto thee.

All souls are thine and, here or there,
They rest within thy sheltering care;
One providence alike they share.

Thy word is true, thy ways are just;
Above the requiem ' dust to dust '
Shall rise our psalm of grateful trust.

O happy they in God who rest,
No more by fear and doubt oppressed;
Living or dying they are blest.
      Alleluia!

1888

EASTER MORN

On eyes that watch through sorrow's night,
   On aching hearts and worn,
Rise thou with healing in thy light,
   O happy Easter morn!

The dead earth wakes beneath thy rays,
   The tender grasses spring;
The woods put on their robes of praise,
   And flowers are blossoming.

O shine within the spirit's skies,
   Till, in thy kindling glow,
From out the buried memories
   Immortal hopes shall grow:

Till from the seed oft sown in grief,
   And wet with bitter tears,
Our faith shall bind the harvest sheaf
   Of the eternal years!

1890

RISEN

They came, bringing spices, at break of the day
  With hearts heavy-laden and sore,
And, lo, from the tomb was the stone rolled away,
  An angel sat there by the door!
'Why seek ye the living 'mid emblems of death?
Not here, he is risen,' the shining one saith.

O type through the ages and symbol of faith,
  Whose spirit is true evermore:
The hearts we have cherished we lose not in death,
  The grave over love hath no power.
There sitteth the angel, there speaketh the word, —
'Not here, they are risen,' in silence is heard.

O ye who still watch in the valley of tears
  And wait for the night to go by,
Lift, lift up your eyes, on the mountains appears
  The day-spring of God from on high!
He turneth the shadows of night into day, —
'Not here, they are risen,' his shining ones say.

Santa Barbara, 1894

WHAT WILL THE VIOLETS BE?

S. A. M.

WHAT will the violets be
   There in the Spring of springs?
What will the bird-song be
   Where the very tree-bough sings?
What will their Easter be
   Where never are dead to mourn,
But brightly the faces ask,
   ' O, when will the rest be born?'

Brighter the Easter shines
   On the faces here below,
That they are behind the flowers,
   The heart of the living glow.
Beautiful secret, wait!
   A morrow or two, and we
Shall know in the Spring of springs
   What the violets will be.

1886

OVER THE LAND IN GLORY

OVER the land in glory
   Breaketh the Easter morn:
Nature repeateth her story, —
   Life out of death new-born!
Lo, the year's at the Spring,
   Buds are blossoming,
     Earth and heavens sing:
Life is life forever, evermore!

Listen, the birds are singing,
   Softly the south winds play;
Bells in the steeples ringing
   Welcome the festal day:
And the message they bear
   On the radiant air
     Chides sorrow and fear:
Life is life forever, evermore!

Skies of the spirit brighten,
　　Hopes like the birds return:
Hearts with the promise lighten, —
　　' Blessed are they that mourn.'
To each winter a Spring
　　God will surely bring,
　　　And the heart shall sing:
Life is life forever, evermore!

Music: ' King's-Chapel Carols,' No. 49. 1890

EASTER FESTIVAL

Lo, the Day of days is here,
Earth puts on her robes of cheer:
Day of hope and prophecy,
Feast of Immortality!
Fields are smiling in the sun,
Loosened streamlets seaward run,
Tender blade and leaf appear,
'T is the Springtide of the year!
    Day of hope and prophecy,
    Feast of Immortality!

Lo, the Day of days is here,
Hearts, awake and sing with cheer!
He who robes his earth anew
Careth for his children too.
They who look to him in faith
Triumph over fear and death;
Speaks the angel by the door
'They are risen' evermore.

> Day of hope and prophecy,
> Feast of Immortality!

Lo, the Day of days is here,
Music thrills the atmosphere.
Join, ye people all, and sing
Love and praise and thanksgiving!
Rocky steep or flowery mead,
One the Shepherd that doth lead;
One the hope within us born,
One the joy of Easter morn!
> Day of hope and prophecy,
> Feast of Immortality!

Music: 'King's-Chapel Carols,' No. 4.   1890

DISCIPLESHIP

On the Judæan hills
   Would I have seen the light
The watching shepherds saw,
   Turning to noon the night?
Would I have seen the star
   That new in heaven shone,
And followed with the few
   The new-born Christ to own?

And if mine ears had heard
   The Man of Galilee
Speaking from heart aflame
   The Truth that maketh free,
Turning from priest and scribe,
   Dead rite and parchment roll, —
Would I have hailed in him
   A Prophet of the Soul?

Those words upon the mount,
   By way-sides, in the town, —
Unwelcome to his time,
   Now Holy Scripture grown, —
Would I have read in them
   A message from on high,
Or joined the multitude
   Who cried out *Crucify?*

Ah, vain for you or me
   To question thus the Past!
Not then but now for us
   The fateful choice is cast;
Ever the larger faith
   Makes way 'mid doubt and scorn,
And in its latest word
   Anew the Christ is born.

The true disciples they,
   The wide earth o'er, who own
Truth in her manger low,
   Ere yet she mounts the throne:
Who from the dead Christ's tomb
   Take not the stones to slay
In blinded fear and rage
   The living Christ to-day.

They hear the angels' song,
 'T is they who see the light
The watching shepherds saw
 Making the heavens bright:
They see the self-same star
 O'er Bethlehem that shone,
And follow joyful forth
 The new-born Christ to own.

1388

THE MAN OF NAZARETH

'A cloud received him out of sight,' —
   Even so; and then men knew no more
The human presence warm and bright,
   As he had walked the earth before;

The preacher of the mountain-side,
   Teaching the kingdom's reign within,
Strong in rebuke of hardened pride,
   Yet pitiful of conscious sin:

But sceptered now, and throned afar,
   They watched in dread his swift return,
To see before his judgment bar
   The earth dissolve and heavens burn.

The gathered clouds of centuries lift;
   No king in wrath descends to reign,
Yet king-like through the shining rift
   The Man of Nazareth comes again.

O Friend and Brother, draw more near
  The while thy festival we keep;
Diviner shall our lives appear
  Held fast in thy high fellowship.

Christmas, 1890

MARY'S MANGER-SONG

Sleep, my little Jesus,
   On thy bed of hay,
While the shepherds homeward
   Journey on their way!
Mother is thy shepherd
   And will vigil keep:
O, did the angels wake thee?
   Sleep, my Jesus, sleep!

Sleep, my little Jesus,
   While thou art my own!
Ox and ass thy neighbors, —
   Shalt thou have a throne?
Will they call me blessed?
   Shall I stand and weep?
O, be it far, Jehovah!
   Sleep, my Jesus, sleep!

MARY'S MANGER-SONG

Sleep, my little Jesus,
   Wonder-baby mine!
Well the singing angels
   Greet thee as divine.
Through my heart, as heaven,
   Low the echoes sweep
Of Glory to Jehovah!
   Sleep, my Jesus, sleep!

Music : 'The Carol,' page 44.   1882

WHITTIER

No thrush at eve had ever sweeter song
Than thine whose voice no more on earth
    we hear ;
Nor winds and flowing streams more please
    the ear,
Nor to the speech of Nature more belong.
And yet thy heart beat ever with the throng
Of toil ; the lowliest life thou didst revere
And the wide law of brotherhood hold dear,
Most mindful still of all who suffered wrong.

Best loved of all the choir we loved so well,
'T was thine to bring again the Master near,
And hymn to men the Goodness without end :
Psalmist we call thee of our Israel,
Child of the Spirit, poet, prophet, seer, —
And to us all, of every name, the *Friend !*

1892

WHITTIER

A RUGGED rock is the mountain,
   Rock from the base to crown;
But the mountain glens and valleys,
   Where the brooks come leaping down,
Are gardens of tender, ferny things,
   Sweet tangles of green and brown.

Like the mountain stood our poet!
   Strength of the hills was he,
In the quiet sky uplifted,
   A moveless sanctity;
And the listening lands heard thunders roll
   Of his Sinai prophecy.

But the brooks in his heart were singing,
   Singing all night and day,
And rhymes like the mosses nestled
   Over the ledges gray,
And a poet's radiant world of flowers
   Out-bloomed from the Yea and Nay.

1892

'NOTHING BUT A POET'

' He sat and talked of his own early life and aspirations; how he marvelled, as he looked back, at the audacious obstinacy which had made him, when a youth, determine to be a poet and nothing but a poet.' — EDMUND GOSSE ON ROBERT BROWNING.

'NOTHING but a poet!' So he said, and wondered
 At the sole persistence of his years.
Laughing world, you'll know it, now that, silence-sundered,
 He is in the welcome of his peers.

What said Milton to him, what said Keats and Shakespeare?
 O, to see the smile on Dante's face!
Catch the great Greek χαῖρε, hear the 'bronze throat' hail him,
 'Browning's come among us, — give him place!'

'Nothing but a poet,' singing songs of soul-
 growth,
Splendor in the pain-throb, rise in fall,
'Saul the failure' in us re-creating kingly, —
 Songs one surge of morning! That was all!

Browning Commemoration, 1890

REMBRANDT

Suggested by the portrait of his mother in the Hermitage, St. Petersburg.

Gazing upon that face where years have wrought
The record of their mingled loss and gain,
Where Love and Death, alternate joy and pain,
Have the hid soul to such expression brought, —
Life fills with vaster meaning to my thought.
'Neath change and loss I read what things remain
To crown at last the struggle and the strain
Of all our days, remembered or forgot.

O mighty Master! Shakespeare of the brush!
Interpreting to eye, as he to ear,

The story of earth's passion and its strife, —
Thy genius caught the new day's morning
    flush,
Saw glory in the common and the near,
And on immortal canvas gave us LIFE!

1892

THE SOWER

'A sower went forth to sow.'

Along the pathless prairie
   The tread of human feet, —
Up rise the smoke-plumed cabins
   'Mid springing corn and wheat.
Where, like a lonely ocean,
   The wind-swept grasses swung,
The golden sheaves are gathered,
   The harvest song is sung.

In vigil of the spirit
   A young-eyed listener heard, —
'Go forth among thy fellows,
   Thy seed the living Word!
By springs of joy and sorrow,
   In fields of toil and care,
Through deserts of temptation,
   Broadcast thy faith and prayer.'

THE SOWER

From year to year the prairie
   Has waved with ripened grain,
Borne on the tides of traffic
   Wide over land and main.
But who shall mart the harvest
   Of nobler thought and deed,
Of holier faith and purpose,
   Sprung from the sower's seed?

O brave and faithful sower,
   Not thine on earth to bind
The full sheaves of thy harvest,
   The growths of heart and mind:
Outspreads in widening circles
   The life-embodied Word,
And they shall bear thee witness
   Thy voice who never heard.

The people cease from labor,
   The children leave their play;
All bring thee love and honor
   To crown thy festal day.

The heavens glow in beauty
Lit by the westering sun,
And God's far stars shall guide thee
When the long day is done.

Chester Covel, Seventieth birthday, 1887

JOHN C. LEARNED

Thy work abides, though thou hast passed
    from sight:
Unconsciously hast thou thy monument
From year to year built fair and permanent
In lives to which thine own was cheer and
    light.
Wisdom and meekness clothed thee with
    their might;
In thee the sage and saint were equal blent;
Strength, courage, tenderness dwelt in thy
    tent,
Thou soldier of the everlasting Right!

By so much as we mourn thee, we rejoice
That we have known thee in these earthly
    ways,
And with thee striven for the things unseen:
Still in our silences will speak thy voice
And thy dear memory inspire our days,
Till we too pass the veil that hangs between.

    December, 1893

'INCARNATE CHEER'

' Have n't I a right to be grave, too, sometimes ?'
J. Ll. J.

No rights of gravity to thee, dear friend!
We need one face about our world to mend
Heart's hurt and set jarred minds in tune,
And sure to do this as the blessed June;
One voice whose bell shall ring away all
    fear;
One hand in which we grasp 'incarnate
    cheer;'
One steadfast smile rayed out from eyes
    alight,
To make men say, 'He's come! now all is
    right!'

  To J. Ll. J. on his birthday, 1887

THIRTY THOUSAND

'Thirty thousand!' said the Fate,
    Mixer of the days to be,
As she passed the mystic gate, —
    Little Quaker baby, she!

Thirty thousand days and nights —
    This the dower with which she came:
All their sounds and all their sights
    Vested in the tiny dame.

'Thirty thousand,' said the Fate;
    But who draw the royal breath
Into deeds the days translate,
    Dainty Queen Elizabeth!

Price is high for royal dowers;
    Thee must *earn* thy golden state!
Spendthrift gods fling out the hours,
    Miser gods keep count and weight.

Day and night and night and day,
 One by one the thousands flee:
Lady of the Yea and Nay,
 Thou *hast* earned thy queenerie!

Earned it as a noble should,
 Dauntless, tireless, gentle-strong;
Giving Yea to every good,
 Daring Nay to every wrong.

Not in calendars thy fame,
 But secrete in happy prayer;
Lips have blessed thee — not by name —
 Thanking God for 'daily care.'

Thou dost leave a sweeter earth,
 Less of poison, less of fen,
By thy precedent of worth
 Stablished in the world's Amen.

Thou art part of all uplift!
 One tint brighter rises morn
Henceforth ever, — this thy gift
 Wheresoe'er a child is born.

To E. B. C., on her eightieth birthday, 1886

GOLDEN WEDDING

WHAT do you see, dear hill-top pair,
Side by side in the quiet there,
Looking down through the golden air
   On the days of long ago?

Sounds of the valley's push and throng,
Din of its labor and cries of its wrong, —
Do they rise and blend to an evening song,
   As you stand and listen so?

Is the valley filling with shadows dim?
Do the hills grow bright on the eastern rim,
The hills where you played so free of limb,
   In the days of long ago?

Tell us your secrets, our two-in-one!
Do fifty years of the rising sun
Draw love the closer for each year run, —
   Will you whisper, you who know?

Beautiful secrets that none can tell
Till sunsets chant and the roses spell, —
As they *do* for twos! as two knew well
   In the days of long ago.

But say, O lover by love long taught,
Why, under the gray the years have brought,
She stands as a *maiden* to our thought,
   And a rose that waits to blow.

Tell us the secret of home-spun ways,
Of spinning-wheel hours in city days,
Clean and calm as a Quaker phrase
   Of the simple long ago.

Tell what you see on the *farther* side,
Where the new horizons open wide,
And you hear the step of a coming Guide
   The way of the hills to show.

Out of the quiet that holds you there
There seems to float through the golden air,
Like the brooding music after prayer
   Or a song of long ago : —

'Little we see ; but hand in hand
Fearless we turn to the still, new land,
Fearless to go as here to stand ;
  For this in our hearts we know, —

'Wherever we go, Love goeth too ;
Whatever may pass, Love lasteth through ;
And Love shall be sweet and dear and true
  As in days of long ago.'

  For J. D. and M. D. : 1836-1886

TWILIGHT

The sunset glow is ebbing;
   Within the rose-rimmed sky
The stars wait wide and lonely
   The slow day's passing by.

The evening dusks the valleys;
   The hill-tops yet are lit;
The shadow broadens upward,
   And the quiet climbs with it.

All that the day dissevers
   Now, in the twilight dun,
Nestles again together, —
   The far and the near are one.

Within her cloistered chamber
   Brooded the evening peace,
As the dear life faded slowly,
   Too happy to wish release.

TWILIGHT

In the widening hush she waited,
   In the beautiful after-glow,
The hills of her memory gleaming,
   The shadows climbing below.

The holy twilight falling
   Was not of the star and sun;
The earth and the heaven lights mingled, —
   And the far and near were one.

O. M. N., 1894

'DEATH AS FRIEND'

After a picture by Alfred Rethel

So still!
The little bird sits on the window-sill;
The sun behind him is sinking slow;
Down below in the city streets
The people are going to and fro, —
    Going home, for their work is done.

    'Tong! Tong!'
    It is vesper-hour,
    And soft strong booms
Steal out from the great cathedral tower
Over the house-tops, over the plain,
    Out towards the sun:
    'Tong! Tong!
Go home, for work is done!'

    The old bell-ringer,
    He, too, is so still!
Fifty years, at the vesper hour,
He has rung the bell in his eyrie tower;

'DEATH AS FRIEND'

A dweller there with the birds in the sky,
In the fields of quiet that overlie
The toil of cities, — ringing ' Peace!
   Go home, for work is done!'

      There, alone,
      Where the undertone
Of the city toil moans up to him,
He has done his part in the busy day,
Ringing the pauses for men to pray, —
Simply, faithfully, fifty years;
Ever, in heart, at his oaken board
Breaking his bread with the crucified Lord,
      In whose great name
      The bells proclaim
' Peace! go home, for work is done!'

      One by one
      The strokes sound on.
He sits in the chair by the window-sill:
The little bird wonders at him so still,
So still in the fingers, so still in the face!
' What ails the ringer?' the people say,
' The vesper-bell rings long to-day:
   We have all gone home,
   And work is done.'

'DEATH AS FRIEND'

Low, low,
In the evening glow,
It tolls and tolls.
In the belfry stands a hooded shape,
With a palmer's shell on his shoulder-cape,
As one who goeth from place to place:
He grasps the rope with a bony hand,
Bending with a tender grace
To each rhythm of sweeping sound.
With a noiseless foot he has climbed the stair,
And touched the old man sitting there,
Waiting for the vesper-hour, and said,
' To-night I ring for you, old friend:
Go home, for work is done!'

So still!
The little bird flies from the window-sill,
The sun has set, and down below
The people are saying, 'It never rang so,
Never before, so sweet and low!'

R. Ll. J., 1885

A. L. G.

1846

So early lost, I cannot tell the lift
Of mother-arms! A toy or two, her gift;
A small white gown, her needle in its seam;
And, dim as is a dream within a dream,
A little figure at a shadow's feet,
Or walking hand in hand upon the street, —
A gentle shadow with an unseen face, —
No smile, no tone, no foot-fall mine for trace:
That is my unknown Mother!

       Yet I know
The inmost currents of my being flow
From her high springs; the faiths that in me
  rise
Have once made happy lights within her
  eyes;

The gardens of my heart are seeded thick
With border-blooms that first in hers were
    quick;
My very thought of God is her bequest,
Sealed mine before I lay upon her breast!

O Mother, could an earthly smile suffice,
And *these* not serve me well to recognize?
Inwrought and deathless tokens pledge us
    joy
What day my Mother meets her grateful
    boy!

1894

ALMA MATER

From many ways and wide apart,
    Obedient to thy call,
Hither we turn with loyal heart,
    Dear Mother of us all!

We walk the well-known paths once more
    Amid the summer's bloom;
We pass familiar thresholds o'er,
    And breathe the air of home.

Nor we alone; they come unseen,
    Unheard their footsteps fall;
Voices long hushed to earth within
    The cloistered silence call.

O, more than gold has been the lore
    We learned beside thy knee, —
The faith that grows from more to more,
    The truth that maketh free;

The strength to do and to endure
  Through good report and ill,
The heart of love, the conscience pure,
  And the undaunted will.

Be proud, O Mother, of thy past!
  It lives in thee to-day;
And still its high traditions cast
  Their light upon thy way.

Our love and hope ring out their chime
  Above thy festival;
Blessings upon thee through all time,
  Thou who hast blessed us all!

1890

THE VILLAGE MEETING-HOUSE

STILL stands the ancient meeting-house
   Upon the village-green,
And white above the circling trees
   The belfry tower is seen.

Uncolored through the simple panes
   The common sunlight pours;
No Gothic arches spring above
   The latched and painted doors.

Their thresholds witness to the tread
   Of feet long since at rest
In yonder field of moss-grown slates
   With Bible-text impressed.

No more at rise and set of sun
   Is heard the numbered toll
That spoke to all the country round
   The passing of a soul:

Yet still with every new-born week,
    Across the meadows fair
And over all the upland farms,
    Sounds the old call to prayer.

I walked again the village street
    By absence made more dear;
That summer Sunday held the bloom
    And fragrance of the year.

I followed with the worshippers
    The ancient house within;
For me with all I saw and heard
    Was mingled what had been.

For memory had new-kindled love,
    And love had quickened faith;
I lived that hour within a world
    That knew not change and death.

I minded not the preacher's theme,
    Nor caught the words of prayer;
My thought had passed within the veil
    And walked with spirits there.

The faithful shepherd of the flock,
   Whose years knew such increase,
Who led in wisdom's simple ways
   And by the streams of peace;

The wise and upright citizen,
   To each good cause allied,
Who brightened more an honored name
   Through all the country-side;

And souls that well had borne their part,
   And little children fair;—
Their unforgotten faces gleamed
   In the illumined air.

I love the minster's vaulted roof,
   Its walls of old renown,
Where sculptured marbles voice the past
   And windowed saints look down:

Nor less I feel our Hebrew strain,
   Distrustful still of art,
That lifts to the Invisible
   Immediate the heart.

For inward more than outward is,
  The soul than any shrine;
Alone our living love and trust
  The altar make divine.

Long may the ancient meeting-house
  Rise from the village-green,
And over all the country round
  Its belfried tower be seen:

Still may the call to praise and prayer
  Be heard each Sunday morn,
And bind in growing faith the past
  With ages yet unborn!

Northborough, Mass.

THE DAYS

In Father Time's old nursery
   The little Morrows wait,
Each one impatient to be out,
   Impatient to be great;
On bravely through the sun to go,
   On bravely through the showers,
A world to see, a Day to be!
   The happy-hearted Hours!

So one by one he lets them out,
   His Days so young and strong,
The morning shining in their face,
   And on their lips a song.
When home they come, their work all done,
   There's quiet in their ways,
And shadows rise and haunt their eyes,—
   They're dear old *Yesterdays!*

And now we love them for the half
    Of all that we hold dear, —
The echo-side of every word,
    The far to every near;
The sunset touch to every hope
    That fades along our skies,
The after-dream, the vanished gleam,
    The love in long-shut eyes.

ROCHESTER : 'Fiftieth Anniversary,' 1892

THE OLD LOVE-SONG

PLAY it slowly, sing it lowly,
   Old, familiar tune!
Once it ran in dance and dimple,
   Like a brook in June;
Now it sobs along the measures
   With a sound of tears;
Dear old voices echo through it,
   Vanished with the years.

Ripple, ripple, goes the love-song,
   Till in slowing time
Early sweetness grows completeness,
   Floods its every rhyme.
Who together learn the music
   Life and death unfold,
Know that love is but beginning
   Until love is old.

Play it slowly, — it is holy
   As an evening hymn;
Morning gladness hushed to sadness
   Fills it to the brim.
Memories home within the music,
   Stealing through the bars;
Thoughts within its quiet spaces
   Rise and set like stars.

For J. W. C. and A. H. C.: 1865-1890

THE DEAR TOGETHERNESS

I DREAMED of Paradise, — and still,
Though sun lay soft on vale and hill
And trees were green and rivers bright,
The one dear thing that made delight
   By sun or stars or Eden weather,
   Was just that we two were together.

I dreamed of Heaven, — with God so near!
The angels trod the shining sphere,
And each was beautiful; the days
Were choral work, were choral praise:
   And yet in Heaven's far-shining weather
   The best was still, — we were together!

I woke, — and lo, my dream was true,
That happy dream of me and you!
For Eden, Heaven, no need to roam, —
The foretaste of it all is Home,
   Where you and I through this world's weather
   Still work and praise and thank together.

THE DEAR TOGETHERNESS

Together weave from love a nest
For all that's good and sweet and blest
To brood in, till it come a face,
A voice, a soul, a child's embrace, —
    And then what peace of Bethlehem weather,
    What songs as we go on together!

Together greet life's solemn real,
Together own one glad ideal,
Together laugh, together ache,
And think one thought, 'each other's sake,'
    And hope one hope, — in new-world weather
    To still go on, and go together!

  Home Dedication, 1891

HERO BY BREVET

I saw a veteran to-day,
With hobbling foot and staff to stay,
In slow march by the window stray.

'What rank?' There was no epaulet, —
Some humble rank that privates get:
The face said, *Hero by brevet.*

'What regiment?' I only know
They take the front where'er they go,
As that were badge enough to show.

'No colors?' None that I could see, —
A few gray locks were waving free,
Like shot-torn banners greeting me.

'In service where?' How could I guess?
No boast of battles marred the dress,
But eyes were full of field-success.

'No scars or maim, no empty sleeve?'
Only the smile that sufferings leave
And weary days and nights achieve.

'And all alone, — no comrade-brother?'
Alone, yet loved beyond all other.
'By whom?'   By men who call her —
    Mother!

1836

NURSERY LOGIC

There in the nursery stood the case,
  Old and battered and brown with age, —
Dear Aunt Ann's with the saintly face, —
  Till one of our toddlers, in cherubic rage,
Chanced on a spring and a drawer flew wide,
And lo, a plain gold ring inside!

Wee Aunt Ann with the mystic smile,
  That was the secret thy eyes held fast!
Did they learn their smile in the long-ago
      while
    When the wooers came and the wooers
      passed,
And not one dreamed that a drawer flew
      wide,
A drawer with a plain gold ring inside?

Nobody guessed from then till now,
  Little maid-aunt, thy secret sweet!
Then nobody *shall*, but he and thou,
  Long in the heaven where old loves meet.
But — knows he yet that a drawer flew wide
To show his plain gold ring inside?

So we all agreed, the children and I,
  Dropping again the ring in its place,
Never to spy what lives so shy
  There in the heart of the old brown case.
But the children say, 'If a drawer flew
    wide, —
There's a dear little uncle and aunt inside!'

Who? is his name. O, *they* know well, —
  Have christened him, wedded him now for
    true!
But that is her secret, and they won't tell;
  So it's just 'Aunt Ann and Uncle *Who?*'
And (bless their logic!) they hear, inside,
Three little dream-cousins who laugh and
    hide.

NURSERY LOGIC

Cousins real to the poets small,
  Brooding the dream, as they themselves;
Christened and charactered, each and all,
  Discrete, insular, untwinned elves!
Poets — or prophets? Should heaven ope
    wide,
Whose are the children at Aunt Ann's side?

1888

HOW LITTLE JO NAMED THE BABY

He stood beside the cradle,
  A tender-brooding care,
Watching with love-illumined eyes
  The baby brother there.

He stood beside the cradle,
  While busily without
The mother plied her morning work
  The happy home about.

Three moons had bloomed and faded
  Since 'Baby' earthward came,
Nor yet with seeking far or near
  Was found a fitting name.

Anon the door was opened, —
  The mother paused and smiled,
As, face all tremulous with joy,
  Up spake the little child:

'Mamma, I've named the baby!'
  'You have? What is it, Jo?'
'I'm going to call him God, Mamma,
  That's the best name I know.'

O depth of heavenly wisdom
  Alone to love unsealed, —
Hid from the wise and prudent ones
  And unto babes revealed!

Wee prophet of the Highest,
  Who touched thy little tongue
To speak so clear the holiest thought
  That e'er was said or sung?

The preaching of the pulpit
  Seems vague and far away,
Beside thy bolder faith that sees
  'Immanuel' to-day.

Ah, well if in each other,
　As through the world we go,
We saw what in that babe was seen
　And named by little Jo!

CLEVELAND, 1886

IN THE ALBULA PASS.

To right, to left, the mountain wall —
   Above, the narrow strip of sky;
And at my feet the Albula stream
   With youth's impatience rushes by.

The air comes cool from snowy heights
   And tonic with the breath of pine;
Around me like a glory spread
   The flowers in rainbow beauty shine.

I leave the cares that weighed me down,
   The heat and burden of the plain;
I feel the strengthening of the hills
   And drink the wine of youth again.

Why thus in haste, bright mountain stream,
   To leave these haunts, so fair to me,
Full soon to find the dusty plain,
   Too soon the all-engulfing sea?

There comes a voice, — the streams can
　　speak! —
　'Fair is my home and youth is free,
And glad my days, yet will I go
　On to the plain, the unknown sea!

'For life is motion and not rest,
　Nor fear I what at last shall be;
The Hand that raised these mountain heights
　Has scooped the hollows of the sea!'

I turn me from the happy stream,
　All bright the years before me lie;
The mountains sink as up I climb,
　And nearer grows the widening sky.

CANTON GRISONS, July, 1888

CORONADO BEACH

The air is tonic with the salty breath
Of coursing billows that at last are free;
Sounds low and sweet old Ocean's symphony,
Whose thought the varying heart inter-
    preteth.
With upturned face and folded palms in
    death
Lies Corpus Christi in mute effigy;
Point Loma, sphinx-like, gazes o'er the sea
Nor heeds the questioning wave that breaks
    beneath.
Along the shore the solemn mountains keep
Their immemorial watch; in yonder town,
Sheltered between them and the curving
    deep,
Unheard the tides of life move up and down.
O peace of Nature! here my burdens fall,
I rest upon the mighty Heart of all!

    SAN DIEGO, February, 1894

DOVER

Mouse-hole in December,
   Quiet little Dover!
What shall I remember,
   Now the days are over?

Snow in hushes falling;
   Blue days creeping by;
Trees in still processions
   Etched upon the sky;
And a silent village
   Where the gray stones lean,
Whispering of a Dover
   They alone have seen.

All I shall remember,
   Now the days are over, —
Mouse-hole in December,
   Quiet little Dover!

When I shall be lying
 With a gray stone over,
Will this great World dim to
 Just a little Dover?

DOVER, MASS., 1886

WE SEE AS WE ARE

The poem hangs on the berry-bush,
  When comes the poet's eye;
The street begins to masquerade,
  When Shakespeare passes by.

The Christ sees white in Judas' heart,
  He loves his traitor well;
And God, to angel his new Heaven,
  Explores his lowest Hell.

1885

TREE-SURPRISE

There 's a rapture in the air,
Thrilling all the branches bare
With the musical vibrations of an unheard
    tune;
Silent trees in winter trance
Feel a something in them dance, —
Then a leaf and bud commotion, and a world
    one June!

There 's a trouble in the air,
And a fog of white despair;
Stiff and black the trees are standing, — are
    they dead, all dead?
In an hour I lift my eyes,
And, behold! a tree-surprise, —
Every twig is flashing crystal from the white
    gloom bred!

> Unheard music in the air,
> Is it rapture or despair
> In my tree of life the Hands will play for this day's tune?
> But why ask it or why care,
> With that gloom-born beauty there,
> And the Hands to play December that shall yet play June?

1885

A DAY IN OCTOBER

I leave behind the crowded street,
   The city's noise and stir,
And face to face with Nature meet, —
   Her happy worshipper.

I walk the unfrequented road
   With open eye and ear;
I watch afield the farmer load
   The bounty of the year.

I filch the fruit of no man's toil,
   No trespasser am I,
And yet I reap from every soil
   And the unmeasured sky.

I gather where I did not sow,
   And bind in mystic sheaf
The amber air, the river's flow,
   The rustle of the leaf, —

A DAY IN OCTOBER

The squirrels' chatter in the trees,
    The sunlight sifted down,
The wholesome odors on the breeze
    O'er ripened harvests blown, —

The hills in distance purple-hued,
    The tinkling waterfall,
The 'deep contentment of the wood,'
    The peace o'erbrooding all.

The maples glow beside the streams
    And fleck the pastures sear,
Like smiles that break from happy dreams, —
    So smiles the waning year!

A beauty springtime never knew
    Haunts all the quiet ways,
And sweeter shines the landscape through
    Its veil of autumn haze.

The blessing of the early rain
    And all the summer's shine
Are garnered in the golden grain
    And purple of the vine.

A DAY IN OCTOBER

What though the groves are silent all,
   No bird within them sings,
Nor on the quiet meadows fall
   Shadows from sunlit wings:

Yet is their summer music part
   Of the still atmosphere, —
So Nature keeps by subtle art
   To sight what pleased the ear.

And all my separate senses seem
   To be but passive keys,
Whereon she plays her world-old theme
   To wondrous harmonies.

I face the hills, the streams, the wood,
   And feel with all akin;
I ope my heart, — their fortitude
   And peace and joy flow in.

Like him of old on Horeb's mount
   I take again my way,
New-strengthened from the healing fount
   Of this October day.

MICHIGAN, 1892

INDEX OF FIRST LINES

	PAGE
'A cloud received him out of sight'	62
A little House of Life	31
Along the pathless prairie	72
A rugged rock is the mountain	67
As silent as the sun-gleam in the forest	29
Bring, O Morn, thy music! Bring, O Night, thy hushes	11
From age to age they gather	40
From many ways and wide apart	89
Gazing upon that face where years have wrought	70
He laid his rocks in courses	46
He stood beside the cradle	106
I dreamed of Paradise, — and still	99
I leave behind the crowded street	117
In Father Time's old nursery	95
I saw a veteran to-day	101
It sounds along the ages	48
Lo, the Day of days is here	57

INDEX OF FIRST LINES

                                                          PAGE

'Mid my life's vicissitude 30
Mouse-hole in December 112

No rights of gravity to thee, dear friend . . 76
'Nothing but a poet!' So he said, wondered 68
No thrush at eve had ever sweeter song . . 66
Not when, with self dissatisfied 33

O Fount of Being's sea 22
O Light, from age to age the same 42
O Lord of Life, where'er they be 50
One thing I do ; the things behind forgetting 35
On eyes that watch through sorrow's night . 51
On the Judæan hills 59
On the rock and girt with ice 14
O Prophet souls of all the years 9
O Thou in lonely vigil led 13
O Thou whose Spirit witness bears 20
Over hills and valleys 26
Over the land in glory 55

Play it slowly, sing it lowly 97

Sleep, my little Jesus 64
So early lost, I cannot tell the lift 87
So still ! The little bird sits on the window-sill 84
Still stands the ancient meeting-house . . . 91

The air is tonic with the salty breath . . . 111
The morning hangs its signal 16

	PAGE
The poem hangs on the berry-bush	114
There in the nursery stood the case	103
There's a rapture in the air	115
They came, bringing spices, at break of the day	52
The sunset glow is ebbing	82
'Thirty thousand!' said the Fate	77
This edelweiss I wear was not first mine	15
Thy kingdom come, — on bended knee	18
Thy work abides, though thou hast passed from sight	75
To right, to left, the mountain wall	109
Unto thee, abiding ever	24
What do you see, dear hill-top pair	79
Whatsoever is just and pure	38
What will the violets be	54
Where men on mounts of vision	44

www.ingramcontent.com/pod-product-compliance
Lightning Source LLC
Chambersburg PA
CBHW020126170426
43199CB00009B/657